Mass *of the* Forgotten

MASS
of the
FORGOTTEN

James Tolan

Autumn House Press

PITTSBURGH

Autumn House Press Staff

Editor-in-Chief and Founder: Michael Simms
Managing Editor: Giuliana Certo
Assistant Editor: Christine Stroud
Interns: Heather Cazad, Noah Gup
Co-Founder: Eva-Maria Simms
Community Outreach Director: Michael Wurster
Fiction Editors: Sharon Dilworth, John Fried
Media Consultant: Jan Beatty
Tech Crew Chief: Michael Milberger

PENNSYLVANIA
COUNCIL
ON THE
ARTS

Autumn House Press receives state arts funding support through a grant from the Pennsylvania Council on the Arts, a state agency funded by the Commonwealth of Pennsylvania, and the National Endowment for the Arts, a federal agency.

ISBN: 978-1-932870-91-6
Library of Congress Control Number: 2013942913

Contents

Mass *of the* Forgotten

The Wind Will Undo Us

and in exchange for what it takes of flesh and dream
return to us the echoes
and fragrance of what we've lost.

The wind does not forget but carries what it can.

My grandfather's voice, the music of his words.
The faint, old country lays he'd hum,
tending the snarl of roses climbing

behind his garage. The thunder I first felt entering

the hollow carriage of my ribs. Sweet olives blooming
and the fresh manure of fields. The first cries
I recognized as passion and as pain.

Her low sighs as I held her beneath the pines.

And the stories the old would tell, while we pretended
to be asleep, of the ones who left
and did not return, the ones

they looked for in our faces while we dreamed

of lost children stolen in the woods
when no one was there
but the wind and a thousand blinking eyes.

I

Red Walls

Where I come from
we take bricks
one by one.

We take them red
and muddied
from the earth.

Where I come from
we take bricks
from the earth.

We take them
one by one.
Where I come from

masons worked.
Ground grew up,
ate what

they left behind.
Where I come from
bricks got swallowed.

And it's our job
to loose them
from the soil.

Where I come from
each takes his bricks
and builds a wall

to protect
what we've been given,
to make special

those we invite in.
Where I come from
the odor of one city

mixes with others
on the wind
that finds its way.

Where I come from
a wolf blows hot
against the walls all day

and bricks are how
we build a home.
Where I come from

hunches grow
from safe places
in the soil, and a soul

builds walls to protect
what must not die.
Where I come from walls

are a kind of flesh
and it's a blessing
to be invited in.

Where I come from
is red bricks from here.

Genius Loci

You are cold and must choose
among shelter, wool, and fire.

Choose the wool. There is much
you do not know. The wind

is strong and cold and there are
those among us waiting

for habits to emerge,
drawing lots as to the nature

of your comfort. We are many,
our patience long. What is it

you truly desire? How long
are you willing to wait? Choose

the wool. Fire burns all night
and you have yet to learn

much of what it means to dwell.

How Far

Among the pines in summer,
a fragrance before the rain.

At nightfall, a silence
between the boughs.

Even the insects of the high
branches are without a sound.

We are only partly dressed
as wind begins to stir

the grass around our knees.
Where is my left shoe?

How far are we from home?

Western Civilization

I think it would be a good idea.
—Mahatma Gandhi

Water runs seaward.
Wind roils and keens.
Home is lifted up
wherever the sky
is long. A child calls.
Fire offers. Flame
gathers fat and ash.
The old grieve what
does not return. Men
hunt wolves wherever
fields green, rain falls,
and oak grow wide.

The land, hollow now.
Nothing left to howl.
The city like
a gleaming cancer
covers what once
was only life.
Green leaves grow
so warily. The dog
no longer bays.
The moon a kind
of memory. His pack
no longer his.

The Forest of My Hair

Twenty-eight in the flesh
but in a mirror all I can see
is a boy after his first crew cut,
five years old and wondering
what happened to his hair,

disbelieving it would ever
grow back, as the barber
and his grandfather promised,
while he wept, silently,
trembling air through his lips,
pointing at his hair
strewn across a tiled floor.

My grandfather unwrapped
sour balls for both of us
and, leaving his Falcon behind,
walked with me to the woods.

These woods, he said, are yours.
They were mine, but I give them
to you. I am old, and it is only right
they should now belong to you.

I have lived most of my life
in the absence
of that gentle voice,

and those woods of mine
were clear-cut years ago,
but my hair,
I wear it long in honor of him.

Sappho, Preparations, and the Moon

I.

The bridegroom comes, taller far than a tall man.

Women wail and gnash their hair, clutch
at breasts that would welcome
his hands, his mouth. They pray
his length might fill them still
and make them round as harvest.

For this they sing a child's song
to the goddess of the tides—

The moon goes up.
The moon goes down.
But mostly the moon is round.

Mostly the moon is round.

II.

Build fast the barricades, carpenters.
Hold back the men whose hands
hunger to snatch
the bride from her procession,
whose mouths long
for the surface of her flesh.

Their bodies want her more
than long years and peaceful lives,
more than marbled meat
or west wind over dead seas.

Her least glance aching
in their haunches, they want her
to ruin their appetites at last
for what is necessary without savor.

III.

Tear the church down. Beam and joist.
Steeple and plank. Tear it down
and build a pyre to roast
those who reek of our desire.

There will be no wedding today.
There will be fire and burnt flesh,
for these are Old Testament times,
and we are the new Jehovahs, gods
of vengeance and small mercies,
who rose from the sea and walked,
our lips salted thick with want.

And none shall have what we will not.
There will be sacrifice by fire
and we will be appeased and without
hunger for a time. Until the next
beautiful children grow new hair

and the old envy groans in us again,
like swans between their thighs.

The moon goes up.
The moon goes down.
But mostly the moon is round.

Mostly it is round.

In the Sacristy

While I unclothed
the body and the blood,
he laid his hand
across my mouth

and from behind
he pressed me
toward the host,

loosened my father's
too-big belt and took
holy oil into his hands
before parting me.

He said nothing as
he eased his finger in
as if anointing there.

He had been teaching us
how Christ took
Thomas into his body
so he might too believe.

He reached his other
hand around
and he softly sang—

I shall see Him,
I shall see Him,
I shall see Him
in His beauty over there;

In His likeness
I'll behold Him
waiting at the portals for me.

When I began to groan,
he turned me
by my hips to him
and kneeled as in prayer,

draped my robes
over him and swallowed
when I came, rose

and preyed on Christ
while I pulled tight
the leather
of my father's belt.

The Gentlemanly Art of Pugilism

I punch you
in the head.

You fall down,
unconscious

but not
quite dead.

Thank you.
It was precisely

the response
I had intended.

On the Subject of Hogs

after D. Gordon Kelly

When surrounded, their first response is to group,
tails together, facing their aggressor.

When the guns report,
they learn from every fallen comrade.

The first, felled between the eyes,
the rest no longer face off directly
but maintain a flanking position.

The next are shot behind the ear,
and the others face nose away
in the farthest corner from a shooter.

There is never justice,
no way to balance carnage with trial.

There is only the meat and what we do
with it, or without, on the killing floor.

Whiskey and the Rake of Mourning

When my father's father died,
  my daddy didn't cry a bit,
just grabbed a fifth of whiskey
  and a rake all bent to shit

then dragged himself out the backdoor
  to do what he did best—
work and drink till the drink was done
  and the work was put to rest.

When he was through, what he had done
  was sheered instead of raked.
The lawn, like a black sheep greened,
  was gone for a dead man's sake,

and the earthen wounds left behind
  gathered a still life of waste,
broken rake and broken man,
  blue-nosed and red-faced.

I hauled his hump into the house
  and poured him to the floor.
The dogs licked vomit from his jowls
  then brayed at the backdoor.

If God is love and father too
  then love is a bare bone.

I left the dogs out in the yard
   and him to rouse his hide alone.

Instead he snored and pissed himself
   there on the kitchen tile,
slack-jawed his partial from his gums
   and bloomed a toothless smile.

Blood Sport

1

When I was a boy, my father would tighten
his stomach and invite me
to punch him as hard as I could.

Pounding away, I'd give him my best shot
again and again. It was useless.
He was invincible, and I was very small.

2

At six, I asked my father if I could marry
Mom when I was older. He was never home.
Why should he care? He only laughed.

3

Still a boy, I raced into the bathroom
while my father was shaving
and belted him right in the gut.

He grunted, doubled over,
and I ran like hell to my mom
only to have her demand that I apologize.

4

Back in the bathroom, I told him I was sorry.
He turned to me, blood trailing down his throat.
I was a man and would marry as I pleased.

2

The Coup

I make a surprise visit home only to discover
my mother is Benito Mussolini,
snorting lines off the bathroom floor

and my father, a skinhead for the IRA,
is sporting Gestapo boots and a mean baldy sour,
marching a Catholic goose-step up and down the hall.

Remembering that history tends to repeat itself,
and not wanting to buck family tradition,

I ask Dad if he wants to haul Benito out back
and string her up like the hog she is. He grins,
says, *Gnarly*, and starts mumbling something
about too much fucking linguine and fascism.

After gutting our dear old matronly dictator,
and other father/son bonding, Dad breaks
into a medley of "Nancy Whiskey" and "Wild Rover."
Touched, I slip him last year's Father's Day letter bomb.

He must have been proud. Martyrdom
had always eluded him.

My Father. Vietnam.

History is not forgetting
my grandparents were not of this country.
I was born an orphan and a bastard
into a world of nuns. A mick and a wop
chose me as their own. Once I had
a mother named Diane
and a father listed only as deceased.
I was born Joseph James Gera,
a name denoting war. The cut
of this jaw, the arch of my brow, the way
my mind weaves the room, the way
I walk and wander, my appetite
for solitude and banter, rigor and a quality
of mercy both scrupulous and calm. What of it
is more than only mine? History is not forgetting
all I have never known—a face quite like my own.

The History of Fresh Fruit in America

The first experience of the new-born banana
is to be sliced of its skin at the very tip
    so as to keep it clean
and diminish the pleasures of blindness,
    an imposed blessing
to be fondled and kissed, squeezed and boffed
until it droops, all puckered and brown,
into some patient mother's dessert bread
    and is served
to the blue-haired ladies of the bridge-club
    in memoriam
of their long lost Carmen Miranda dreams
of fruit-topped chiquita dancing
    to exotic latin rhythms
before the big one, WWII, the good war,
when the men who were men fought far away
and dreamed of Betty Grable thighs
and the creamy white children that slid out
all shiny and clean
    into our brave new world
of Eisenhower, Ford, and the actor Reagan,
Three Stooges' fingers in your eyes
    until they made you laugh
at Protestant work ethics and Catholic morality
checked at the door of Birdland
and filtered through Beat San Francisco hookahs

into the rock 'n' roll, love, and hash
        of the Haight
ménage à trois, fucking in slow motion,
with Vietnam and Charles Manson,
        until my father
wore a body bag home from the war
and my mother saved her unwed soul
by giving her first born away to the nuns
to grow up in some confused Medieval circus
of free love and guilt,
        tracing Bob Marley out of death
back into adopted big band records
of white folks singing,
        Yes, we have no bananas today.

A Sense of Community

We live in a world
of wiggly worms,
and you, sir,
are a wiggly worm,

and wiggly worms, sir,
are the lowest form of life,
coming out of everywhere
with nowhere left to go.

And I, sir,
am a wiggly worm
of limited means
and uncertain ancestry,

and if, sir,
you were to chop me in half,
I'd move away from you
in opposing directions.

And if, sir,
you were to hunt
the two of me down
and proceed

to chop
and chop again,

there would be
a community of me,

waiting to circle
back upon you
when you
were least aware,

for you, sir,
are a wiggly worm,
and I, sir,
am a nation.

Raising Christ

Lou, sweet Lou, hooch drinking, poke pinching,
    unslovenly, veracious, heart's rain of a woman,
    drip dripping honey wine from her lips to my
    pearly gate-mouthed face on the barroom floor.

Is this the first taste of the second coming, the scent
    that remedies a rough beast's slouch, pulls him
    erect and hopeful out of Bethlehem to our new
    world?

No Holy Spirit or heavenly host has caught the musk
    of her flesh on the wind and seeks her out now to
    redeem him, to convince him to come again.

He's been waiting 2000 years without knowing it was
    Lou he needed, that it was Lou, caterwauling in
    the wilderness of the West, calling him back to
    the one life twice born between her thighs.

The second time around he comes as more than his
    father's son, as a god who must learn to be a man,
    and it's Lou who knows the way,

sweet Lou, the Magdalene, whose feet he must learn
    to wash, whose feet he must learn to take into his
    mouth and love, Lou, whose skin covers the heat

of a moist and leaky soul, Lou, who knows the
new covenant is born by a man, who just happens
to be god.

Charred

I didn't want you in that burned-out building last night
because I wasn't ready to share you with the sky,
the curious eyes of the moon and stars,

because I wasn't man enough to come out loud
with pants around my ankles, my hands
cradling your ass in the empty window sill,

because I was scared to want you riding me
beside roach shit in the malt liquor stench,

scared to want my tongue between your legs
as you leaned against a smoke-stained wall.

I didn't want you in that burned-out building
because I wasn't ready to give up your scent to the wind,

because my cock would have been
so hard our screams would have brought the cops,
because our juices would have drowned your fine new shoes,

because we might have burst into rain,
and you are too hard to find beneath the earth.

I didn't want you that lost and randy night
charred with possibility
because there was nothing I wanted more.

In the Nick of Time

I was lost

and this poem

found me.

Now we're lost

together.

Giggles before the Void

I could take her ass
and put it in a box by the window

and every morning I'd open the box
and tickle her ass with a goose feather

and giggle

but sooner or later she'd want it back
and I'd be stuck with an empty box

and a bald goose

and every morning I'd have to get up
and feed that goose

and look for something to put in the empty box.

Celebrating Our Anniversary

We sit across from each other
staring sideways at

She twists her hair,
wets her lips as if to

I look up,
begin to ask

She leaves to pour a drink.
I skulk off to bed.

The next morning
she's curled beside me.

I leave to draw a bath.
Matted hair clots the drain.

I scrub that tub until it shines
and walk quietly back to bed.

We sit across from each other
staring sideways at

I Ate Your Pancakes

like the pumpkin pie and orange
zest muffins with wheat germ
and bran. So many treats
you have fashioned of late,

and I have eaten, ravenous
for the hunger and passion
I was sure you had buried inside
each bite. But your hunger and passion

were so well hidden,
only their fragrance remained.
And when I traced it back to you,
offered a hand to shoulder or to thigh,

it was clear. The secrets are yours.
I am lucky to have the food.

Red Grown

He doesn't recognize her
without her cloak and blush

but she cannot forget
who first treated her like food.

His smile, when she takes him
to her cottage in the woods,

perhaps he wishes it
were tender, hopes she will be

a taste of heaven in the flesh,
a spring lamb born to slaughter,

but as soon as he paws
her ruddy belt, she

will carve across his gullet
a smile more sincere

then roll him from her bed,
his carcass, limp and fat

as a belly full
of undigested grandmother.

3

The Wrong Ones

There are those who make us sad,
maybe not at first; maybe at first

we love them and have been waiting
to love them all our lives, but maybe

they're really only second chances
to love those we had neglected

to love before—our mothers
and lovers, fathers and strangers—

and maybe we were right
not to love them the first time;

maybe our love was holding out
for a world of its own choosing

and those who make us sad now
make us sad because we're loving

the wrong ones, the ones we'd hoped
would grow smaller as we walked away

instead of showing themselves again
in those we have failed to love anew.

Corpus Poetae

I love a boy
who will not breathe.

Each morning
I feed my breath to him.

His sigh is slight,
but it is all

I need to go on.
My breath no longer mine,

I save all I can for him
and have forgotten

what else there was
to love.

I eat little
and have grown thin,

but my breath is sweet.
Each morning he sighs,

or so it seems,
and I am happy in my way.

And I am not.
It is all we have, all

a man so wed
can reasonably hope.

I am pale with love
for that boy

whose mouth
is almost warm.

Always tomorrow
I will leave him,

and always
tomorrow dies

into no one
to breathe for today.

Half a Man Loves a Woman in Two

I wanna touch her
but her skin's too tight.

I try 'n' kiss her
but her mouth ain't right.

I swore I loved her
and she split in two.

One half don't love me
but the other half do.

The half that loves me
stays inside the door.

The half that doesn't,
don't live here anymore.

A Murder of Crows

I came home to a murder of crows
perched along the gutters of the house,
filling the trees up and down the street.

Then with a bang, they were gone.
A neighbor lighting firecrackers
said the crows bothered his dog.

I explained that crows were sacred birds
revered as the bearers of strong omens
since long before the time of Christ.

He sighed and moved to light another,
so I killed him and joined my brothers
and sisters, now returning to the trees.

Caravaggio's Thomas

I.

There are four of us in robes, looking
at where the lance had been.
I am the one in front,

leaning over, owl-eyed
and furrowed, index finger
halfway in the opening

beneath Christ's right nipple.
Not a wound exactly,
there is no blood or gore,

just a hole, a small, lipless
mouth lodged in the middle
of his ribs. Christ, always teaching,

guides my right hand,
as if a patient were showing
his doctors a new way

into the body, as if
God could show a man
how to love his own wounds.

II.

He drew me in between his ribs,
his hand on mine more gentle
than any had ever been.

It hurt how tender he was.
I couldn't feel
my finger going in.

How could I feel
what wasn't there?
It was like faith,

my finger halfway in and him
not making a sound.
He was supposed to be dead,

and I was supposed to know
better than to believe
that he had been,

my finger entering,
perhaps,
the skin and bones of God.

Should You Die,

don't come back to me
as some fixed object

to be met
with shallow breath

but as a breeze
at my bare neck

when I forget
how much I loved

when you were breathing.

Drear Heaven

Wing I have lost—sheen
of gloss-black feathers furled
against what drear heaven is

promised augury's truants and spare parts.

I the crow—single-winged
and stumbling
amid ripe carrion and dreck—

a ground bird, flightless and about to die,

bitter sure but wishing
my lost wing well, imagining
it in flight above fields rich

with what remains after harvest.

Yielding to hunger and the earth,
it might return. If only
I can last until the thaw, maybe

it will miss me too,

my caw and wary eyes, the perfect
fit of my shoulder, empty
socket from which it flew—

undressed gore gone dry.

The Meat Course

The fork rising to my mouth is something more
than etiquette and its tapered tines.
It is the four-pronged stake that carries
the remains of another

whose life becomes my own,
a pitchfork diminished
in the service of we who cull
sacrifice from a menu of palatable tropes,

the minor edifice of civility we impose
against the plain necessity of death
and the digestion of its corpse.

Devil Born

The widower wanted for his love
     a burial: proper, Christian
and offered handiwork or summer harvest
       in exchange, but sacraments are costly
         business, and this preacher
was not one to coddle the parish poor.

     She had been a faithful servant
of the congregation, but her farmer husband
      would have to pay cash or bury her
      near animal bones behind the barn.

     The way back home went on and on.
He could barely see for wind and snow
      then fought what sleep came that last night
       with her wrapped beside him.

Near dawn he began to chop the frozen mud,
        where she would be
buried beneath the juniper she loved.

He felt the plaque within his heart begin
      to harden like the gristle
   of week-old bacon between his ribs.

     His spade made four feet down before
he hit ground he could not break. Anything

more shallow than the length of a tall man
and she would float with the spring floods.

Bent over creaking knees, he tore
from icy earth and stone
a wooden box the size of a cow's heart
he heaved against the hard bottom of her grave.

Rusted hinges snapped. The chest
erupted gold. Head bowed to his wife's god,
he clasped rough hands and trembled
slow tears into the stubble of his beard.

He wrapped their boon
in a threadbare blanket beneath their bed
and brought her body to the preacher once more,
handed him a fat stack of coins
which bought the finest funeral to be had
in those poor and barren parts.

After the burial,
amid dried flowers, cashews and candied fruit,
the preacher could hold
his tongue no more and asked
how the farmer had come to own such coins.

Artless, the codger shared his story
with the preacher who divined
a way to make that treasure his.

He commanded his wife to slaughter
her milk goat and bring him its fresh hide,

unwashed at the horns, had her whipstitch
        the skin along his shoulders, arms, and back,
                along his neck and crown.

        Cloaked under warmest robes he stole
to the old man's ramshackle in the night
where he shed his outer garb and lit
squat candles on the ground. Rapping quick
and hard against the widower's bedroom glass,
                he claimed the treasure his.

        The farmer paid no heed until
                the costumed preacher claimed
the dead wife would be a whore of Hell
        for all eternity unless
                what remained of devil's gold
                was returned that moonless night,
for a funeral bought with Hell's currency
was no sacrament in the eyes of God.

                The old man unlatched the door
and chucked the chest outside. The devil gathered
        gold into his robes and turned
                churchward one last time.

Cut this skin from me, he ordered his wife,
        ashen as the gray of milk,
and with each snip her sewing shears drew blood.

        He snatched the scissors from her hand,
                then whimpered as new blood fell.
The goatskin and his own, no difference anymore.

The Darkening of the Host

What is there to recommend a life on high
beyond the grandeur of an eloquent

descent? Perfect hair and not a callus
on the harp-worn hand? The hauteur of a God,

omniscient and conditional, brandishing
the daily succor of a fruit, tasteless and unforbidden?

Downstream

My uncle Tommy used to drink
a lot, and I loved him for it.
He'd bring me gifts I didn't know I wanted—

How & Why books on Indians, aircraft, and fish,
a drafting set, colored pencils and pastels,
Classic Comics, a pen pal sister from Vietnam.

He'd teach me, but only when he was drinking,
how quickly an earthworm could reproduce
by slicing one we'd freshly dug in two,

how to draw the dying of an autumn field
and weed the wild places behind the sunflowers
with a machete bought on shore leave in Hong Kong.

Otherwise, he'd spend hours in his room,
alone with sober memories
of a broken marriage and child long years gone,

sketching half-built houseboats, women
in pedal pushers, walking along a shore,
children on swings, forever waiting to be pushed.

Fifteen years since his liver finally called it quits,
I look at a photo the size of a business card:
silly felt hat drooping over his eyes,

he rows downstream, bare-chested and smiling,
toward no place in particular. I sit across from him
now, in no particular hurry to arrive.

4

The Purple Crayon

I find a jumbo Crayola in the new used couch—purple
like in *Harold and the Purple Crayon*, the children's book
I once believed was named after my dad—and I'm sixteen again,
driving him home one more last time from the bar
at Ted's Log Cabin, where he's been since lunch,

closing in again on the indoor martini record, double digits
no big thing, when, stopped at the corner of Lewis and Grand,
he flings open his door and lets loose all over the road.
No usual drunken puking, this one's laced
with bloody coagulum, olives, bifocals, and false teeth.

I throw the two-tone Dodge into park, fish his specs
and teeth out of the mess and drive him to St. Therese
and two weeks in detox before the next new lifetime
of *Hi, I'm Hal T and I'm* . . .

                    My dad's story and a crayon,
a lie I've been telling for almost twenty years.

My mother was driving. It was one of the few times
she wouldn't go get him by herself. She is the one
who dipped into what his body emptied
to rescue the only help he'd ever admitted needing,
she who drove him to the hospital, who stayed with him

despite all those drunken years, who loved him more
than I have ever known how to love. I'm thirty-two
and still want to be the hero, want to be the one
reaching into the retch, the one making the necessary
gesture, not the pimpled boy in the back seat,

mouth hung wide, unable or unprepared to act—
Hamlet still considering the ghost.
I loved my father and did nothing, sat there,
hating myself for loving this chance to see what I'd
been hiding and holding inside all those years.

Kiss

Cling to something you can imagine and believe,
something without feathers or angel's breath,
but hope all the same,

what we loosen from our hands
to become what we will in the end.

Miracles do not cease:
the mandolin and summer peach.

Follow the old roads.
They lead to what remains—

the savored blessing
of a dying father's ragged sigh,

the loss of some floating childhood
we held against helium and the wind.

Loose your grip from that taut string
and live at the tattered edge of all
we have ever known of this, love's blackest kiss.

Chicago 1942

to my father

Every day they pulled
the boxcars squealing
up to the stockyard gates.

Each pig-packed car
contained its own lead hog

over whose head
they slipped a loop
of coarse hair rope
before they dropped a boy.

Hold on, they snapped
as they whacked its ass
and sent them bolting
toward the gates.

A bar just overhead,
grab hold
and the nickel was yours,

miss,
and the rest of the hogs
would not.

Hands wrapped
round rusted iron,
you always held on.

What choice did you have?

Breath Robins

for my father

You lie down on a lawn of fresh-cut grass
and bury your face among its blades.

Rising, you are one among a subdivision.
Flame-breasted birds nest in the gutters behind your ears,
cukking for the tender meat of worms.

The wind breaks and your skull cleaves
open beneath the razor of its cutting breath.

Robins flock to the teeming attic above your eyes,
where they feast on the fleshy
wind-bared morsels cluttering your new airway.

A View to the South

The rooms of the house are yours alone.
You know all the furnishings, the placement
of details, but the room to the south
is strange. You can't seem to recognize

the view through the windows.
A walled garden fallen to ruin, a path
leading out to a darkened wood, the smell
of fresh water in the distance, all this

calls to you. And the man cast in shadows,
charting your way on the old map
hung for decoration on the wall, waits
for no one but you, ashes fallen at his feet.

Sacrifice

At the factory where people watch machines press dough
into wafers the size of a Roman coin

a man works who has been saving
his communion wafers for years, holding them

in his mouth until safely back at the pew
where he seals them in Baggies he smuggles home

in hope of piecing together the mystery
of his lord's body on a cross laid out in the garage.

The Wind at Rest

A man rises
after tumbling
down a hill of clover.

He is the wind
at rest among
the places where we lie.

Alone in a theater,
bored into dreaming
his hair on fire,

people come to gaze
at what laps
above his head.

It will be years
before he thinks
to watch

the flames
reflected
in their eyes.

Returning Home

after long work,
two corbies
and a dove
cut a pale sky.

In the clutch
of each black bird
a relic
of their supper,

for one a clump
of golden hair
to thick
their high, dark nest.

The other carries
like The Fates
a blue eye
freshly plucked

from one who will
not need it now,
born light
and clear as air

by the dove
who spirits him—
west wind
through bare, white bones.

The Return

An old man sits in my straight-backed chair
salvaged from the curbside trash
sits quietly, without shifting or harrumphing,

sits and drinks plain tea, his sober eyes
never doubting what his life's been worth
or who he has become.

I wait for him to swallow
one more slow sip of tea, before I ask
where he has been so long without me.

Inheritance

My grandfather had a special fork
whose tines bent wide to hold
as much scungilli pasta as he could fit
into his wide Italian mouth.

I can still see him shoveling it in,
slurping and licking his lips, slugging
Fortissimo and laughing, smiling
at all of us, his family before him
at tables spread across the yard.

Sunday dinner, my mouth
open wide in *compagnia di comari*,
panting with laughter, I see him
in their eyes. Who can be alone,
chi sarebbe solo, among so many?

Cemetery Plums

One who would offer ripe fruit to the dead
as if knowing their desires, believing
desire still lived in them, would know

how tangible remains the memory
of its juice across the mouth and chin
and sliding along the tongue.

Do not be misled. The dead miss life
more than we miss them, their loss
more than equal to our forgetting and our grief.

And a bowl of fruit offered in their name
returns to them as the memory of a mouth
rapt in joy around moist and living flesh.

Who among the dead does not long
for the sun-wet meat of a smooth-skinned plum,
the bitter sweetness of each pitted heart?

Acknowledgments

Thank you to the editors of the following publications in which these poems appeared—

American Literary Review: "The Wrong Ones"

Atlanta Review: "The Forest of My Hair"

Autumn House Anthology of Contemporary American Poetry: "Blood Sport," "Giggles before the Void," and "The Purple Crayon"

Bellevue Literary Review: "Cemetery Plums" and "Western Civilization"

The Best of Bellevue Literary Review: "Cemetery Plums"

Coffeehouse Poetry Anthology (Bottom Dog Press): "Blood Sport"

Connecticut Review: "Chicago 1942," "Kiss" (as "Without Feathers") and "On the Subject of Hogs" (as "Active Shooter Survival Tips")

december magazine: "My Father. Vietnam."

Enchanted Conversation: "Red Grown"

Fairy Tale Review: "Devil Born"

On the Dark Path: An Anthology of Fairy Tale Poetry (13 Moons Press): "Red Grown"

Family Matters (Bottom Dog Press): "The Purple Crayon"

Fogged Clarity: "How Far"

The Fourth River: "Breath Robins" and "Half a Man Loves a Woman in Two"

Fulcrum: "The History of Fresh Fruit in America"

Gargoyle: "Corpus Poetae"

Good Foot: "Giggles before the Void"

In the Garden of the Crow (Elektrik Milk Bath Press): "Red Grown"

Indiana Review: "Blood Sport"

International Quarterly: "Genius Loci"

J Journal: "A Murder of Crows"

Knockout: "The Coup" and "A Sense of Community"

Lake Effect: "The Darkening of the Host"

Lilliput Review: "In the Nick of Time"

Linebreak: "Inheritance"

Louisiana Literature: "Should You Die,"

Many Mountains Moving: "Sacrifice" (as "Sacrament")

Margie: The Journal of American Poetry: "The Purple Crayon,"
    "Red Walls," and "Whiskey and the Rake of Mourning"

New America: Contemporary Literature for a Changing Society
    (Autumn House Press): "The Purple Crayon"

Poetry in Performance 37 (City College Press): "Blood Sport"

5x5 Postcard Series (Purgatory Pie Press): "The Gentlemanly
    Art of Pugilism"

Quiddity: "The Meat Course" and "The Wind Will Undo
    Us" (as "The Wind in Time Will Undo Us")

REAL: "I Ate Your Pancakes" and "The Return"

Red Brick Review: "A View to the South"

Rock and Sling: "Caravaggio's Thomas" and "Raising Christ"

The Windsor Review: "Celebrating Our Anniversary"

Two Weeks: A Digital Anthology of Contemporary Poetry (Line-
    break): "Downstream"

What Have You Lost? (Greenwillow Press): "The Forest of My
    Hair"

A number of these poems appear in *Red Walls* (Dos Madres Press)
and *Fresh Fruit and Gravity* (Far Gone Books).

Thank you to the Atlantic Center for the Arts, Poets House, the Professional Staff Congress-City University of New York Research Foundation, and the Borough of Manhattan Community College for opportunities important to the making of this collection.

And heartfelt thanks as well to those who did so much to make these poems better: Sheryl St. Germain, Darrell Bourque, Lucien Stryk, Robert Bly, and Robert Creeley first and then Fran Quinn, Owen Lewis, Estha Weiner, Myra Shapiro, and Jason Schneiderman of late. To Michael Simms and Autumn House for shepherding this book to press with such heart and care. To Junuh who woke me. And to Holly who makes wonderful more than she can ever know.

The Autumn House Poetry Series
Michael Simms, General Editor

Unreconstructed: Poems Selected and New	Ed Ochester
Rabbis of the Air	Philip Terman
The River Is Rising	Patricia Jabbeh Wesley
Let It Be a Dark Roux	Sheryl St. Germain
Dixmont	Rick Campbell
The Dark Opens	Miriam Levine • 2007, selected by Mark Doty
The Song of the Horse	Samuel Hazo
My Life as a Doll	Elizabeth Kirschner
She Heads into the Wilderness	Anne Marie Macari
When She Named Fire: An Anthology of Contemporary Poetry by American Women	Andrea Hollander Budy, ed.
67 Mogul Miniatures	Raza Ali Hasan
House Where a Woman	Lori Wilson
A Theory of Everything	Mary Crockett Hill • 2008, selected by Naomi Shihab Nye
What the Heart Can Bear	Robert Gibb
The Working Poet: 75 Writing Exercises and a Poetry Anthology	Scott Minar, ed.
Blood Honey	Chana Bloch
The White Museum	George Bilgere
The Gift That Arrives Broken	Jacqueline Berger • 2009, selected by Alicia Ostriker
Farang	Peter Blair
The Ghetto Exorcist	James Tyner*
Where the Road Turns	Patricia Jabbeh Wesley
Shake It and It Snows	Gailmarie Pahmeier*
Crossing Laurel Run	Maxwell King*
Coda	Marilyn Donnelly

• Winner of the annual Autumn House Poetry Prize

* *Coal Hill Review* chapbook series

Design and Production

Text and cover design: Chiquita Babb

Author photograph: Louis Chan

This book is typeset in Truesdell, a font designed by Steve Matteson in 1994, based on the original design drawn by Frederic Goudy in 1930

This book was printed by McNaughton & Gunn on 55# Glatfelter Natural